Recapture Your Finances 2.0

By Bina Artiste

100% Canadian

Enhanced Version

Copyright © 2024 by Bina Artiste. 862228

All rights reserved. No part of this book may be reproduced or transmitted in any form or by any means, electronic or mechanical, including photocopying, recording, or by any information storage and retrieval system, without permission in writing from the copyright owner.

This is a work of fiction. Names, characters, places and incidents either are the product of the author's imagination or are used fictitiously, and any resemblance to any actual persons, living or dead, events, or locales is entirely coincidental.

To order additional copies of this book, contact:
Xlibris
844-714-8691
www.Xlibris.com
Orders@Xlibris.com

ISBN:	Softcover	979-8-3694-2826-9 (sc)
	EBook	979-8-3694-2825-2 (e)

Print information available on the last page

Rev. date: 08/27/2024

Dedicated to...

My father, my mother, my sister,

my brother, Tommy,

and Nermall Allan Em.

Book Cover: Made by Bina Artiste using the Canva app

Other Books to Read:

Debt-Free Forever by Gail-Vaz Oxlade (January 3, 2012)

[2014 AuthorHouse.com] Treasures Of Light & Darkness by Bina Artiste Chauhan

[2015 AuthorHouse.com] Of Jewels and Gems by Bina Artiste Chauhan

[2019 AuthorHouse.com] Sliver Moon by Olivia South

[2019 AuthorHouse.com] Gr0und Zer0 by Bina Artiste

[2019 Xlibris.com] F.R.E.E. by Bina Artiste

[2023 Xlibris.com] Heavenless by Bina Artiste

[2024 Xlibris.com] Recapture Your Finances 2.0 by Bina Artiste

They say to save while young... Any age is good to save.

How?! You might ask?!

Let me skip the boring introduction and skip the boring chapters, and dive right in. Here are financial secrets I have learned by trial and error, by being a professional accountant in my field, a business owner of YFL – Youth For Life, and hefty amount of budgeting. I started budgeting anally ever since I rented my first bachelor apartment at 25 in the heart of downtown Vancouver, BC, Canada on Nelson and Denman. I started building my Net Worth in 2018.

Budget 1.0

Here is a small example of a budget I do every cheque I get, be it big or small. (I use an Excel spreadsheet on my computer.)

Budget – August 21, 2024

1600.50	Persons With Disabilities designation (PWD)
243.06	TFSA (12%)
700.00	Beauty by Apple
202.00	Xtra Loan pmnt
250.00	New Phone
102.72	Visa Credit Card
102.72	Emergency
425.00	Business Income from Tommy
387.50	Rent
37.50	Hydro

PWD

Persons with disabilities can apply for a monthly source of income and make up to $16,200 as a single person before the monthly income is deducted dollar for dollar and then stopped until February of the following year.

TFSA

Tax-free Savings Account is a great way to save! You can save up to $95,000 tax-free and can withdraw anytime without being penalized.

Beauty by Apple

Okay, let's face it. We all need to pamper ourselves. Most salons would charge double for getting fake dreadlocks. But it is my friend's business and she gives excellent rates for me.

Xtra Loan Pmnt

My only true debt is a consolidated loan and right now it is $9133.29. I try to make an extra loan payment every month of $202 or $101 depending on my budget with my business income and employment. I find those are good numbers to work with for me.

New Phone

So my Iphone was stolen, and Tommy is a big Samsung user so I bought a cheap Samsung A04e version for $200, and I find it does way more. Siri is Google Assistant. I am upgrading my phone to Tommy's old phone Samsung S20 and he is getting the Samsung A21 Fan Edition. And then I am selling the A04e on Facebook Marketplace for $200 because I still have the original box and it's still in brand new condition. I take care of my phones. I love that the Samsungs have a customizable alarm for the days of the week and future dates.

Credit Cards

At one point I ended up with 5 credit cards and managed to pay off 4 and close the accounts. Now I only have the one Visa that I manage. I love this Visa because I accumulate points and every 5000 points I get $50 towards TFSA's. And when I make a payment through the same Credit Union account, the money is instantly there. I try to pay it off in full as soon as I make a day of purchases. I also reduced the credit limit from $3000 to $2500 so I am not tempted to spend more.

Emergency Funds

I actually have 2 emergency accounts. One for regular emergencies and one for my brother's emergencies. Born with a blue heart and having to get open heart surgery as a baby, he was destined to be fucked for life. So Tommy and I have a emergency account for him.

In Order

First comes:

12% TFSAs (pay yourself first)

Rent

Bills (including hydro, gas bill, phone, internet, food and Visa)

Emergency Fund

Personal pleasures

Pie Chart 1.0

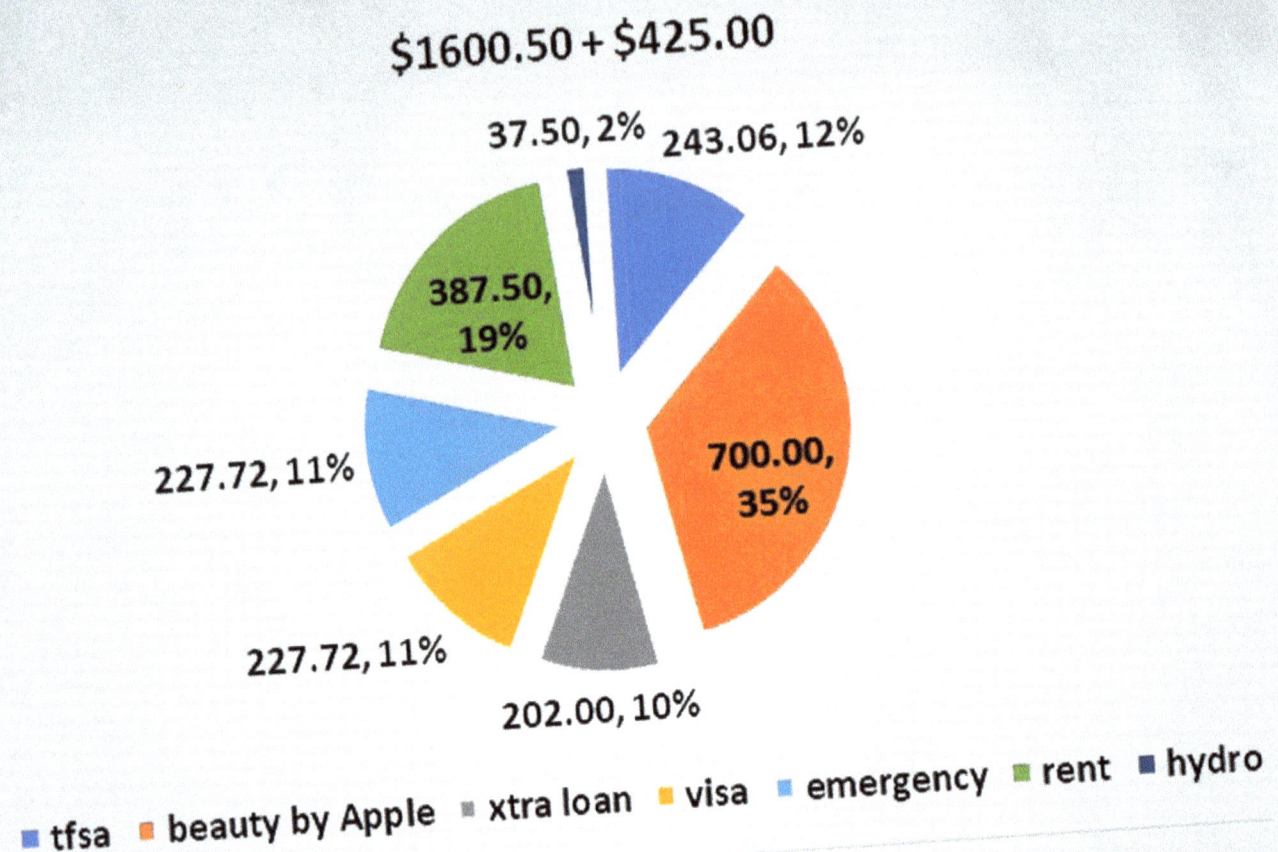

Business

One great way to make money is to start up your own business. I started with Avon Canada because a friend was selling it and she stopped so I joined online and ever since then it's been almost perfect.

I say almost, because my eldest sister purchased $5000 worth of products from me, after I signed her up. Then she lost her job and didn't pay me. My business almost went under, but I had good support to write it off my taxes as a loss, and my best sister forced evil sister to pay me back. I also lost my leadership status since all my sign-up leads quit. It's better not to do business with family. Needless to say she's banned from the family.

But other than that I have been able to write off all my receipts for the year 95%. I registered my business with CRA (Canada Revenue Agency) as Youth For Life. So I brand everything YFL.

I also have my own manufacturing line and labels. I create and sew clothing, purses, cat quilts, bookmarks, and envelopes. On Sundays I go to the flea market and set up a table with my own branded tablecloth and a mixture of Avon and YFL products.

RDSP's

RDSP's, or better known as Registered Disability Savings Plan, is available at a starting $11,000 from the government of Canada, if you are on PWD persons with disability income. Every dollar you invest into your RDSP fund, the government matches times 3. You can invest and contribute until you are 49, and the money is accessible when you are 59.

I actually had to cash in my RDSPs early due to my cancer and a shortened lifespan.

Rent Subsidy

Before I got serious about savings, Rent was the first thing to come off my budget. But now I know I have to pay myself first (TFSAs 12%)!

Rent subsidies are hard to get now, but if you have one keep it. A rent subsidy means the company paying your rent will pay it in full to your landlord and in return you pay $500 to the said company.

Luckily Tommy and I had a last minute plan when we were getting evicted from our last place. The landlord kept wanting to increase the rent illegally and Tommy kept showing her the provincial rules. Needless to say it pissed the landlord off. So I was convinced I needed to find a place of my own Tommy said, "Nevermind you, I am going to save my own ass!" and looked online for cheaper living options that were mobile. I saw the RVs and said hey, that's a great idea! And luckily I had an RRSP of $10k from a past employment pension. I was allowed to withdraw it with a medical note from my doctor about my cancer and bought a 1 bedroom RV. And our rent is only $387.50/mo each.

Hydro

In the Winter I budget $50 for my half and in the Summer, I budget less as we don't have an air conditioner, $37.50. We have 5 fans running full blast all day and it is way less electricity. Plus Tommy installed full LED lights throughout the RV. My last half of the Hydro bill was $25.27.

We don't have propane, just electricity. We are planning on getting a new RV with 2 bedrooms, 2 bathrooms and it's the same size! And we bought everything to set up solar panels on the roof. It's a great thing Tommy is a great handyman.

Disability Bus Pass

I used to work for transit so I got a free pass through my work. It was great for 7 years, as I use buses and Skytrain all the time in Metro-Vancouver. And luckily I was part-time there so I had disability insurance as back-up. And disability insurance has $52/month unlimited pass.

Employment

Now, I know most people don't want to work. They want everything for free. Or they would rather drink and do drugs. I, on the other hand, love to work. It's my passion and drive. I work for a Canadian phone company as a Customer Service Technician from home and I love it. Plus I have started contributing to RRSP matching retirement plan. Hey, nothing beats free money, eh?

But sorry honey, "You work hard for your money, and we're going to treat you right." Money needs to be respected and not abused. There are millions of liars and thieves and scammers. Don't be one of them.

Budget 2.0

Budget - March 29, 2024

$1062.35	Employment Income	
$127.63	12% RRSP Pension	Mar 29
$225.00	Tommy Payroll Cleaning	Mar 29
$126.34	Loan Payment	Mar 30
$202.00	Xtra Loan Payment	Mar 29
$38.08	Phone Plan	Apr 11
$171.65	Visa	Mar 29
$171.65	Emergency Fund	Mar 29

Savings

I can't tell you enough. Savings! Savings! Savings! TFSAs! RDSPs! RRSPs!

<u>Pie Chart 2.0</u>

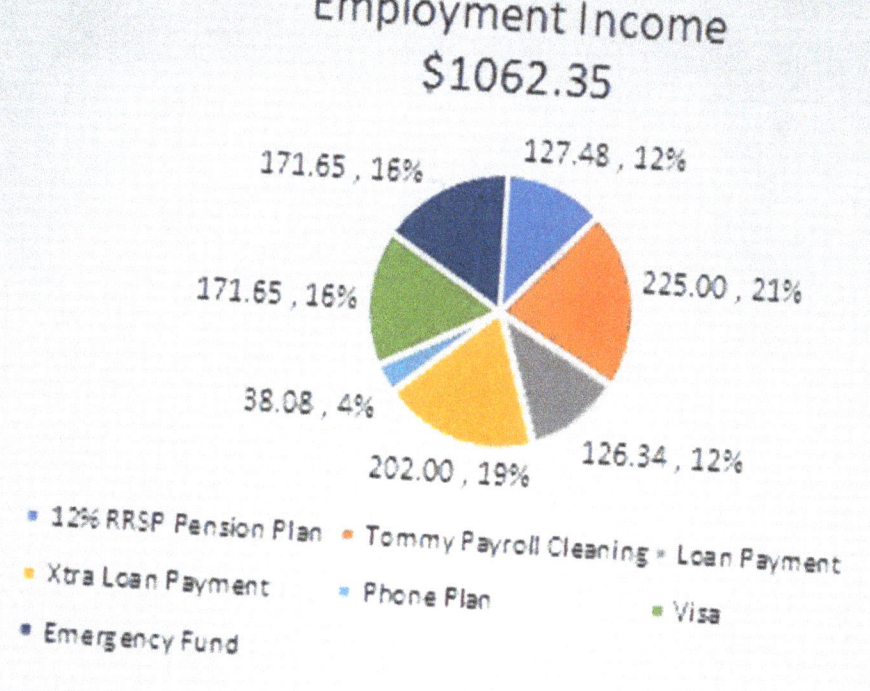

Poverty

I would love for you, dear reader, to get out of poverty like I did. I was almost homeless, begging for cigarette butts and food on the streets. I am so glad I met Tom. He helped me to pull myself out of poverty, by encouraging me to take my medications on time and to save my money.

www.ingramcontent.com/pod-product-compliance
Lightning Source LLC
Chambersburg PA
CBHW040545220526
45473CB00016B/3025